MW01128647

KidChat
Oh, the Places to Go!

The KidChat Series

KidChat
KidChat Too!
KidChat Gone Wild!
KidChat Oh, the Places to Go!

The Question Guys™

KidChat
Oh, the Places to Go!

204 Creative Questions
to Let the Imagination Travel

Bret Nicholaus and Paul Lowrie

A Deborah Brodie Book  Roaring Brook Press * New York

*For Josh and Shannon
and all the places you will go*

Text copyright © 2007 Bret Nicholaus and Paul Lowrie

A Deborah Brodie Book
Published by Roaring Brook Press
Roaring Brook Press is a division of Holtzbrinck Publishing Holdings Limited Partnership
175 Fifth Avenue, New York, NY 10010

All rights reserved

Distributed in Canada by H. B. Fenn and Company, Ltd.

Library of Congress Cataloging-in-Publication Data

Nicholaus, Bret.
Kidchat, oh the places to go! : 204 creative questions to let the imagination travel /
Bret Nicholaus and Paul Lowrie. — 1st ed.
p. cm.
"A Deborah Brodie Book."
ISBN-13: 978-1-59643-317-5
ISBN-10: 1-59643-317-5
1. Children's questions and answers. 2. U.S. states—Miscellanea—Juvenile literature. 3. United States—
Miscellanea—Juvenile literature. 4. United States—Description and travel—Juvenile literature.
5. Curiosities and wonders—United States—Juvenile literature. 6. Games—Juvenile literature.
I. Lowrie, Paul. II. Title.
AG195.N534 2007
031.02—dc22

10 9 8 7 6 5 4 3 2 1

Roaring Brook Press books are available for special promotions and premiums.
For details, contact: Director of Special Markets, Holtzbrinck Publishers.

Book design by Mikael Vilhjálmsson
Printed in the United States of America
First edition October 2007

welcome again!

It's 2,824 miles from Los Angeles, California, to New York City, New York; it's 2,092 miles from International Falls, Minnesota, to Miami, Florida. In between these U.S. extremes you'll find national parks and amusement parks, big-city skyscrapers and small-town surprises, beautiful beaches and majestic mountains—oh, the places to go! With this exciting collection of KidChat questions (written, as always, to get kids thinking creatively and talking enthusiastically), kids will journey all over this great land. In addition to the questions—all of which deal with U.S. geography and/or vacations in some way—are fun and fascinating bits of kid-friendly travel trivia scattered throughout the book. As a result, kids learn about interesting things to see and places to visit in the United States while using their imagination to answer geography-themed questions.

Since there is no specific order to the questions, kids can open the book to any one of the 200-plus questions and start right there. Sometimes they might go through three or four questions in a few minutes; at other times, one question will lead to a 15-minute dialogue. There is no way to predict where these thought-provoking, fun questions will lead; in fact, a question might be answered one way today and completely differently tomorrow!

Regardless of whether this book is used in the classroom, at the dinner table, or in the car (a likely possibility given the theme of this book!), kids will have a blast providing their own unique answers to these entertaining questions. And as always, we encourage adults to join in the fun. Besides discovering that you have some pretty good creativity left in you, we have a feeling you'll learn some pretty cool stuff too. (For instance, did you know that the second-most visited home in the United States after the White House is Graceland, Elvis Presley's former home in Memphis, Tennessee?)

Happy answering!

Bret Nicholaus and Paul Lowrie, The Question Guys™

P.S. Are we there yet?

special note

Every 15 questions or so, kids will notice a heading that says "imagination igniter." These words indicate that the question below it is specially designed to stimulate very creative thinking and the full-blown use of their imaginations.

Washington

Montana

North Dakota

Oregon

Idaho

South Dakota

Wyoming

Nebraska

Nevada

Utah

Colorado

California

Kansas

Arizona

New Mexico

Oklahoma

Texas

Alaska

0 120 240   480 Miles

THE UNITED STATES OF AMERICA

— 1 ←

The likenesses of Presidents George Washington, Thomas Jefferson, Abraham Lincoln, and Theodore Roosevelt are carved into the side of Mount Rushmore in the Black Hills of South Dakota.

WHICH ONE OF these great men would you like to have a one-on-one conversation with? What would you talk about?

— 2 ←

IF YOU COULD visit the birthplace or childhood home of any American who is now deceased, whose would it be?

3

MOST LARGER cities—and some smaller ones—have descriptive nicknames, such as the Mile High City for Denver, Colorado. What would be a clever nickname for your hometown?

4

IF YOU COULD turn a minivan into the ultimate touring machine, what feature would you add that is not currently found in one of these vehicles?

5

Head south to Canada? That's exactly what you do in Detroit, Michigan, by taking a tunnel ride under the Detroit River!

IF YOU COULD have any country in the world just a few miles from your house, which one would you want as a neighbor?

6

IF YOU COULD DO anything at all to a typical hotel to make it more exciting for kids to spend the night there, what would you do to it? (You can't say, "Add an indoor water park," because lots of hotels already have them. Be creative!)

7

During the summer, water temperatures at Myrtle Beach, South Carolina, are in the 80s, while during the same time of year water temps in Los Angeles, California, are in the mid 60s.

IF YOU COULD be whisked away to a sandy beach right now, what would you do there?

8

IF YOU COULD jump from place to place to have the perfect vacation day, what specific things would you want to do from the moment you woke up until the moment you fell asleep from exhaustion?

9

What a climb! There are 893 steps to get to the observatory at the top of the Washington Monument, 555 feet and 5⅛ inches above Washington, D.C.

WHAT IS THE highest number of steps you've ever climbed?

10

IF YOU COULD choose a brand-new place to serve as the nation's capital, which city would you choose and why?

11

IF YOU COULD shout anything at all from the top of the highest mountain in the United States, Alaska's Mount McKinley, what would you say?

12

WHAT IS THE tallest natural or man-made object you've stood beside?

13

The only physical evidence of the Lewis and Clark Expedition is near Billings, Montana. William Clark's name and the date July 25, 1806, are carved into a butte called Pompey's Pillar.

IF YOU COULD spend 3 days in any section along Lewis and Clark's route, which part would it be?

14

IF YOU COULD travel back in time, what year would you go to and what place would you visit? Why?

Imagination Igniter

→ 15 ←

The smallest park in the world is only 452 square inches, and it's in the median of a road in Portland, Oregon! Originally a weed patch, over the years it has featured oddities such as a swimming pool for butterflies and a miniature Ferris wheel.

IF YOU COULD have your own miniature city park, what would you place there for the public (or local wildlife) to enjoy?

— 16 —

WHAT IS YOUR favorite place to visit that is more than 100 miles away from your home, but not farther than 500 miles away?

— 17 —

A tradition of the Indianapolis 500-Mile Race in Indiana is to present the winner with a bottle of milk (plus a wreath and a trophy).

IF YOU JUST WON a major car race and were presented with a bottle of some type of liquid, what would you want to guzzle in your moment of glory?

18

HIGHWAY SIGNS often let travelers know what's ahead—for example, construction, a sharp curve, gas stations, restaurants, or train tracks. If you were to create a sign to let people know what you think lies ahead in your own life, what would your sign say? What symbol would you use to depict it?

19

OUT OF THE 7 regions of the United States, which one would you prefer to live in: New England, Mid-Atlantic, Midwest, South, Southwest, Mountain, or Pacific?

At Crater of Diamonds State Park in Murfreesboro, Arkansas, you can dig for diamonds—and keep what you find!

IF YOU FOUND a handful of diamonds in the rough, what would you do with these gems?

IF YOU COULD have any 2 states, with all of their current geographical features and cities, bordering your town on 2 sides, which ones would you want to be only a bicycle ride away? Why?

22

MOST STATES have a welcome sign that greets motorists as they cross into the state. If you could design a new welcome sign for your state, what would it look like? What would it say?

23

THE STATUE OF Liberty in New York Harbor stands tall as a symbol for freedom. What freedom in America are you the happiest to have?

24

IF YOU COULD have a kid-sized version of any American city, which one would you want to make kid friendly? Why?

25

MISSOURI IS known as the Show Me State. If you could show all of the kids in the world something you own, what would it be?

26

JUST ABOUT EVERY state has a nickname, usually because of something it's known for. If you could give your home state a new nickname (whether or not it has one already), what would it be?

27

Berried Treasure, Jamaican Me Crazy, and Fossil Fuel are just a few of the outrageous combinations made at the Ben and Jerry's Ice Cream Factory in Waterbury, Vermont.

IF YOU COULD create your own ice cream flavor, what would you name it and what would you put in it to make it a wild taste sensation?

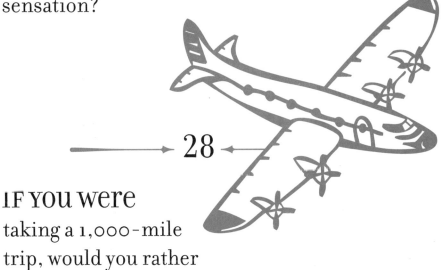

28

IF YOU WERE taking a 1,000-mile trip, would you rather drive or fly to your destination?

imagination igniter

→ 29 ←

IF YOU WERE stranded on a remote highway in the middle of nowhere but knew that help would reach you in 4 hours, what would you do to pass the time?

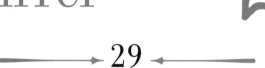

—— → 30 ← ——

IF YOU COULD create a hot-air balloon in any shape, what would it be? (After you build it, you could take it to Albuquerque, New Mexico, where the world's largest hot-air balloon festival is held each October.)

—— → 31 ← ——

WHAT LANDMARK, geographical feature, or site would be the most incredible to view from a hot-air balloon cruising 1,000 feet above the ground?

— → 32 ← —

IMAGINE THAT a new state were being admitted into the Union and you were asked to choose a name for it. What name would you give it?

— → 33 ← —

Mount St. Helens in Washington State erupted on May 18, 1980, removing more than 1,000 feet of the mountain and destroying almost 230 square miles of forest!

IF YOU KNEW that you could safely witness a natural phenomenon, which one would you like to watch unfold close up?

— 34 —

WHAT IS THE most awesome road you've ever been on? What made it so cool?

— 35 —

On Cannon Beach in Oregon, a sand-sculpting contest is held each June. Several teams are given a 20-foot-square plot of sand to create a sculpture that will only last a day!

IF YOU ENTERED a sandcastle-building contest, what masterpiece do you think you could realistically sculpt in a few hours?

36

IF YOU COULD have a beach made of anything other than sand, what would you want to feel between your toes?

37

WITH 3,099 MILES of roadway, Interstate 90 is the country's longest interstate. If you were to cruise the entire stretch—from Massachusetts to Washington—what kind of vehicle would you want?

—— → 38 ← ——

SOME STRETCHES of interstates are downright boring! What attraction would you build just off an interstate to pull in travelers for an afternoon?

—— → 39 ← ——

IF YOU COULD visit the White House, what would you be most interested in seeing? If you've already been there, what particular feature would you enjoy seeing again the most?

IMAGINE THAT you could
have any national landmark
completely to yourself for a
day. Which one would it be
and what would you do there?

IF YOU COULD change the color of San
Francisco's famous Golden Gate Bridge
from orange to something else, what color
would you paint it?

42

HOW WELL DO YOU know the 50 states? Pick a state at random and find out the thing it is best known for (such as Idaho and potatoes).

43

Rhode Island is the smallest U.S. state, measuring only 37 miles wide by 48 miles long.

IF YOU COULD carve out a new small state that was only 25 miles square, where would you place it within the current borders of the United States?

44

IF YOU COULD make any state twice the size that it already is, which state would you want to double?

Imagination Igniter

→ 45 ←

World's fairs entertain, educate, and inspire visitors from around the world by allowing them to explore other cultures and view scientific advancements and new inventions. But there hasn't been a world's fair in the United States since the one held in New Orleans in 1984.

As the lead planner for a new world's fair, what types of things would you want people to know and see? What American city would you choose to host it?

46

IF YOU WERE designing a postcard of your area, what would you put on it to represent the sights tourists would want to see?

47

If you stand at the top of Mount Katahdin in Maine, you can see the sun rise before anyone else in the United States!

WHAT IS ONE thing that you routinely like to do before anyone else does it (things like finishing your supper, taking your bath, or doing your homework)?

— → 48 ← —

OF THESE 5 natural places—canyon or gorge, large cave, remote island, mountain, waterfall—which would you choose for a first-time visit?

— → 49 ← —

SOME U.S. TOWNS are the biggest producers of something: for example, Akron, Ohio, is known as the Rubber Capital and Hatch, New Mexico, is the Chili Capital. What would you say your hometown is the capital of and why?

50

IF a HUGE tractor-trailer truck could bring you a truckload of anything you wanted from anywhere in the United States, what would you want this 18-wheeler to deliver to your home?

51

THE STATE OF Texas is huge, and Texans, being proud of that fact, like to have the largest of just about everything (for example, Texas toast). If you could make any one item in your home Texas-sized, what would it be and how much larger would you make it?

52

HOW MANY CITIES in the United States have populations of more than 1 million people? (Consult an atlas and have fun finding out!)

53

IF YOU WERE IN charge of developing a new 500-mile stretch of interstate, what would you do to the interstate—or to points along it—to make the ride really fun?

54

THE UNITED STATES is filled with a vast amount of natural wonders: canyons, forests, lakes, mountains, rivers, and rock formations. Of all the famous American natural sites you can think of, which one would you like to have right outside your back door?

55

The wettest spot in the world is Mt. Waialeale in the Hawaiian Islands, where an average of more than 460 inches of rain falls in a year!

HOW WOULD YOUR life be different if it rained all the time where you live?

56

IF YOU COULD create the perfect weather for a 1-week family vacation, what would it be?

57

The Birmingham Civil Rights Institute in Alabama memorializes the achievements of people who brought about equality for African Americans and strives to promote civil and human rights worldwide through education.

WHAT INEQUALITIES do you see around you that should be overcome?

— 58 —

WHAT CITY IN THE United States do you want to visit more than any other?

— 59 —

IF YOU HAD TO carry a suitcase with you everywhere you went and it always had to contain the same things, what would you put in it?

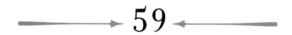

IMAGINATION IGNITER

→ 60 ←

LET'S SAY THAT you've just inherited an abandoned ghost town, plus a million dollars to revive it. What would you spend the money on in order to bring your town back to life?

— 61 ←

Mammoth Cave in Kentucky is the world's longest cave—more than 350 miles of passages have been mapped so far!

DO YOU THINK IT would be fun to live in a cave? Why or why not?

— 62 ←

THE FAMOUS song "America the Beautiful" is full of phrases that express the amazing beauty of this vast country. What visually descriptive phrases can you create that capture the beauty of the United States?

—————→ 63 ←—————

All rivers east of the Continental Divide flow eastward;
all rivers west of the divide flow westward.

IF YOU WERE a river, would you rather
flow east or west? Why?

—————→ 64 ←—————

IF YOU COULD GO whitewater rafting on
any river in the country, which one would
you pick for your water-soaked adventure?

65

The borders of Utah, Arizona, New Mexico, and Colorado come together in a single point where you can touch all 4 states at the same time.

HOW many different states have you been to so far? Which ones?

66

IF YOU COULD visit any relative in your family who lives far away, whom would you most want to visit? Why?

67

Horses that have won the Kentucky Derby often have unusual names, such as Smarty Jones, Funny Cide, Charismatic, and Real Quiet.

IF YOU ENTERED a horse in this world-famous race, what unique name would you give it?

68

IN YOUR OPINION, what do you think would be the most exciting place in America to visit?

— → 69 ← —

THROUGH THE National Park Service's
Volunteers-In-Parks program, people have
donated 5 million hours or more each year
to help the national parks. What national
park is closest to you and how would you
volunteer to give it a hand?

— → 70 ← —

WHAT WOULD YOU rather sleep in for
a couple of nights in the great outdoors, a
tent or a camper?

———————→ 71 ←———————

Oregon's state flag is the only one that has a different design on each side!

IF YOU WERE designing a new state flag for your state, what symbol would you use as the centerpiece?

———————→ 72 ←———————

WHICH STATE DO you think has the coolest-sounding name?

→ 73 ←

If you swam in Great Salt Lake in Utah, you'd be almost unsinkable due to its high salt content!

IF YOU KNEW that you couldn't sink, which body of water would you choose to swim across?

→ 74 ←

IMAGINE THAT you're on the local tourism board for your town. What slogan would you create to entice visitors?

Imagination Igniter

→ 75 ←

The Outer Banks is a 100-mile long chain of islands and sandy reefs along North Carolina's northern coast. More than 2,000 ships have sunk in this area, earning it the nickname Graveyard of the Atlantic.

IF YOU were on a ship with all of your possessions and were told that the ship was sinking and that you could only save a single thing, which item would you grab as you headed for a lifeboat? Why?

→ 76 ←

IF YOU WERE given an island on which to build anything you wanted, what would you build there?

→ 77 ←

The Ak-Sar-Ben Rodeo in Omaha, Nebraska, gets its name from spelling Nebraska backward!

WHAT IS YOUR state's name spelled backward?

→ 78 ←

IF YOU COULD take one ride from any amusement park in the country and relocate it in your own neighborhood, which ride would you choose?

→ 79 ←

ONE-THIRD OF all the states' names start with the letter M or N. If the United States were to add a new state and its name had to start with M or N, what would you suggest as a name for the 51st state?

80

IF YOU VISITED your favorite state and could take home only one single souvenir, what would it be?

81

About 150 wild ponies graze along the beaches of Assateague Island's Chincoteague National Wildlife Refuge in Virginia.

IF YOU COULD have an entire island all to yourself but had to share it with a bunch of one kind of animal, which species would you want as your neighbor?

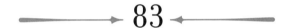

82

what is the longest drive you've ever taken? The most boring? The most exciting?

83

Motorized vehicles are banned on Mackinac Island in Michigan.

if you and your family had to do without the family car for a month, how would your daily life change? How would it improve? How would it become worse?

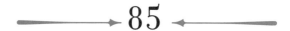

84

IF YOU COULD aDD a special feature to your family's car that would make long road trips more exciting, what would it be?

85

At the World of Coca-Cola in Atlanta, Georgia, you can taste more than 70 different beverages that aren't available in the United States.

WHaT WOULD YOU add to your favorite soft drink to make it your own special blend of flavor excitement?

86

IF YOUR PARENTS allowed you to bring 3 friends along on your next family vacation, which ones would you choose?

87

Cleveland, Ohio, is the home of the Rock and Roll Hall of Fame and Museum.

IF YOU COULD GO back in time, which famous musician would you like to meet and watch perform live?

— → 88 ← —

IF YOU COULD move north, south, east, or west of where you currently live, in which direction would you want to move? Why?

— → 89 ← —

The Hollywood Walk of Fame in Los Angeles, California, has the names of celebrities from the entertainment industry embedded in stars in the sidewalk.

IF YOUR hometown had a walk of fame honoring local people for the great things they've done, whose names do you think should be in it?

imagination igniter

→ 90 ←

IF YOU HAD TO move permanently to another state, which one would you choose? Why?

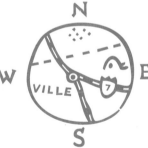

91

All U.S. interstates and highways going north and south have odd numbers, and those going east and west have even numbers.

IF YOU COULD create a new highway, what number would you give it and in which direction would it take you?

92

OF ALL THE places you've visited so far, which one was the most memorable? Why?

— → 93 ← —

Mount Washington in New Hampshire has the highest
recorded wind speed in the world—231 miles per hour!

WHAT IS THE windiest event you've ever
experienced?

— → 94 ← —

IF YOU COULD place a 10,000-foot
mountain anywhere in the country and
gaze down from the top of it, where would
you put it?

95

HOW many Rhode Islands would fit into the state of Texas? (To figure it out, divide the landmass of Rhode Island into the landmass of Texas. An atlas will give you the sizes of both states.)

96

IF YOU COULD take a single state and divide it into 2 separate ones, which state would you choose to split up and why?

97

The International Peace Garden on the North Dakota/ Canada border celebrates peace between nations.

IF YOU COULD create a special garden or park for people to visit, what would it celebrate?

98

IF YOU WERE a tour guide, what tourist attraction would you want to learn more about and discuss with others all day long?

→ 99 ←

Due to Alaska's rugged terrain and lack of roads, 1 in every 36 Alaskans has a pilot's license!

IF YOU HAD a pilot's license and could fly anywhere on a moment's notice, where would you go?

→ 100 ←

WHAT DO YOU think is the most interesting attraction within 200 miles of your home?

→ 101 ←

Two forms of music are American originals. Jazz was born in New Orleans and the blues in Mississippi.

IF YOU WERE IN A band, what type of music would you play?

→ 102 ←

MANY HIGHWAYS are named after famous people. If you could have a highway, or a portion of one, named after you anywhere in the United States, where would you want that stretch of road to be?

103

Wisconsin is known for its dairy cows, yet 90 percent of the milk they produce is used to make cheese!

WHAT IS YOUR favorite way to enjoy milk (for example, in cheese on a pizza, in ice cream, in a milk shake)?

104

WHAT PLACE THAT you've never been to do you look forward to visiting most of all?

Imagination Igniter

→ 105 ←

Carhenge, on a highway outside of Alliance, Nebraska, is a sculptural replica of England's famous Stonehenge. But instead of huge stones it has cars stacked or placed on end.

WHAT KIND OF gigantic sculpture would you like to make out of someone else's junk?

→ 106 ←

IF YOU WERE IN charge of designing a summer camp just for kids your age, where would you want the camp to be located and what types of activities would you want the camp to offer?

→ 107 ←

Where can you find $90 billion in gold? Fort Knox, Kentucky, that's where!

IF YOU HAD EVEN $1 million in gold, what are the first things you would buy with it? How much would you be willing to share with others?

→ 108 ←

IF YOUR CLASS were to make a field trip to a place that was an hour away from school, where would you want to go?

→ 109 ←

It takes 5 million steps to hike all 2,174 miles of the Appalachian Trail!

WHAT IS THE longest walk you've ever taken?

—— → 110 ← ——

IF YOU COULD take a hiking trip anywhere in the United States, where would you most want to go exploring?

—— → 111 ← ——

Miss America is crowned each year in Las Vegas, Nevada.

IF YOU WERE IN A pageant that featured a talent competition, what special skill would put you ahead of the other competitors?

—————→ 112 ←—————

IF YOU were asked to create a brand-new car game for people to play when they're traveling, what would the new game be? How would it be played? What would it be called?

—————→ 113 ←—————

There are plenty of beautiful lakes in this country—Minnesota alone has 11,842!

IF YOU COULD create the perfect lake setting for a vacation, what would it look like?

114

IF YOU OWNED a boat, where would you want to sail it? What would you name it?

115

Many zoos feature pavilions dedicated to insects. Kansas State University in Manhattan, Kansas, however, has an insects-only zoo!

IF YOU COULD create a small zoo for a single species, what would it showcase?

— 116 —

IF YOUR PARENTS allowed you—and you alone—to plan a 1-week family vacation, where would you go and what would you do? (Be specific.)

— 117 —

One of the oldest and largest state fairs in America is held in Des Moines, Iowa, every August.

IF YOU COULD create a competition to be held at a state fair, what would it be? Would you compete in it? Could you win it?

— → 118 ← —

WHERE IS YOUR favorite spot to
go when you just want to be alone?
Why do you like going to that
spot more than any other
location?

— → 119 ← —

Want to visit a place that's truly delicious? Try Hershey,
Pennsylvania, home to the Hershey Chocolate Company.

WHAT IS YOUR favorite way to enjoy
chocolate?

imagination igniter

→ 120 ←

---

when you go on vacation, you leave your routine life behind. What is one thing that you don't miss doing while you're on vacation, yet drives you crazy not to do when you get back home (for example, playing video games)?

— 121 —

Two Connecticut port cities are associated with submarines. Groton is home to the largest submarine manufacturer in the United States and nearby New London to the largest submarine base in the world.

IF YOU COULD take a submarine ride below any water surface, what body of water would you want to explore?

— 122 —

HOW many states do you think you could name from memory in 30 seconds? (Okay, now try it and find out.)

123

Many towns across the United States are named after countries. In Indiana, for example, you can visit the towns of Mexico and Peru—they're less than 6 miles apart!

IF YOU COULD rename your town after a country, which country would you choose?

124

HOW many towns in your state are named after countries? Depending on where you live, you may be surprised to find out just how many there are!

→ 125 ←

New York City is home to more than 12,000 yellow cabs that will take people anywhere for a fare.

IF YOU COULD instantly summon—and pay—someone to provide a service for you, what task would you like to have done?

→ 126 ←

IN YOUR OPINION, which of these historical modes of travel would be the most enjoyable: a covered wagon, a horse, a riverboat, or a steam-powered train?

127

MANY CITIES feature beautiful fountains as part of their landscapes. If you could build a fountain as a focal point in a large city in your state, what would you do to make it different and inspiring?

128

IF YOU COULD take any landmark or geographical feature from another state and move it to the area where you live, what would it be?

129

Maryland's state song, "Maryland, My Maryland," is sung to the tune of "O Christmas Tree."

IF YOU CREATED a new state song for your state, what familiar song would you use for the music and what words would make up the main chorus?

130

WHAT PARTICULAR feature would you like to add to a standard road map or atlas to make it more interesting to read?

131

At 726 feet, the Hoover Dam on the borders of Arizona and Nevada is the highest dam in the United States. It took about 4½ million cubic yards of concrete to build it.

IF YOU WERE given that much concrete to use in a building project, what mega structure would you build? (Remember, that's a lot of concrete!)

132

IF ALL OF YOUR family members came along, what do you think would be the most enjoyable way to pass 2 hours in the car on a road trip?

→ 133 ←

Graceland, Elvis Presley's former home in Memphis, Tennessee, is the second-most visited home in the United States after the White House in Washington, D.C.!

WHICH FAMOUS person's home do you most want to visit?

→ 134 ←

What color is the White House? White, of course.

IF YOU COULD paint it a different color (and rename it after that new color) what color would you choose for the home of American presidents?

IMAGINATION IGNITER

→ 135 ←

The beaches of Grand Haven State Park in Michigan sing! (The "singing sand" emits a whistling sound when it's walked on.)

IF YOU COULD hear a sound come from any surface you walk on, what would you want to hear? Why?

— 136 —

WOULD YOU rather spend a weeklong vacation at the beach or camping in the woods?

— 137 —

Promontory Summit, Utah, is the place where the Central Pacific and Union Pacific railroads met and were joined with a golden spike on May 10, 1869, creating America's first transcontinental railroad.

WHAT IS ONE technological feat you would like to see accomplished that has not yet been achieved?

— 138 —

IF YOU COULD travel around the United States by train, what particular part of the country do you think would be the most exciting to view from the observation car?

— 139 —

Missouri and Tennessee are surrounded by 8 states—the only states that have so many neighbors!

HOW WELL DO YOU get along with your neighbors?

— 140 →

WHICH OF THE 2 noncontiguous states (meaning not connected to the other states) would you rather live in if you had to: Alaska or Hawaii? Why?

— 141 →

As many as 20,000 people run in the Boston Marathon each year.

IF YOU COULD create any new type of race, what would you race and where would it be held?

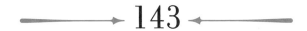

142

WHAT IS THE most unusual activity or strangest thing you've ever done on a vacation?

143

Wenatchee, Washington, is known as the Apple Capital of the World: 15 percent of the nation's apple supply comes from this area!

IF YOU COULD have an unlimited supply of one kind of fruit tree growing in your town, what would you choose?

—— → 144 ←——

IF YOU COULD add any new themed park or hotel to Walt Disney World Resort in Florida, what theme would it be and what unique feature would dazzle its visitors?

—— → 145 ←——

IF YOU COULD own any piece of land in the United States, which one would you want to call your own?

146

WHO'S THE snoozer and who's the talker in your family? On a long road trip, who do you think would sleep the most? Talk the most?

147

Swedish settlers built the first log cabins in the United States in Delaware in 1638.

IF YOU COULD build a house from anything in nature other than tree trunks, what would you use to construct your natural dwelling?

148

IF YOU COULD live in a house that was built in the shape of any of the 50 states, which one would you like your house to look like? Why?

149

Each year the Chicago River is dyed green as part of Chicago's annual St. Patrick's Day celebration.

IF YOU COULD safely but impressively modify one natural feature around your hometown for a day, what would you change?

IMAGINATION IGNITER

→ 150 ←

As a passenger, how much influence do you really have as far as where you get to go?

151

IF YOU COULD live in any famous monument, such as the St. Louis Arch or the Washington Monument, where would you like to wake up each morning?

152

WHAT ONE monument or building in America do you think symbolizes this country the best?

153

Alaska has many kinds of animals, but no snakes—it's too cold for these reptiles!

IF YOU WERE camping in the great outdoors, what animal would make you least excited about roughing it?

154

IF YOU HAD TO choose a big city, a historical site, or a national park for a vacation, which one of these types of places would you pick? Why?

155

Located in Wyoming, Montana, and Idaho, Yellowstone is America's first national park.

IF YOU COULD protect any acreage in the country, which land would it be and why?

156

IF YOU COULD SIT around a campfire in any national park, which one would you like to be in and what scenery would surround you?

157

The Cascade Tunnel in Washington State's Cascade Mountains is the longest railroad tunnel in the United States—7.8 miles long!

IF YOU COULD tunnel your way under anything at all, what would you want to dig under?

158

MANY KIDS—and adults—are fascinated by train rides. If you had to plan the route for the ultimate 10-mile train ride, what sites, natural and man-made, would the train go past? (Be as creative as you can with this one.)

159

The world's first Ferris wheel appeared at the 1893 World's Fair in Chicago.

IF YOU COULD design any new amusement ride that would be fun for the entire family, young and old, what fun way would you have to transport people?

160

IF YOU COULD create the ultimate water park, what types of attractions would it feature and what would be the park's overall theme?

Georgia is the nation's number 1 producer of three Ps: peanuts, pecans, and peaches.

IF YOUR STATE could be famous for producing any one thing at all, what would you want it to be?

IF YOU COULD create a tourist trap for your area, what would it feature?

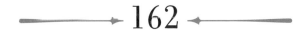

163

With a surface area of 31,820 square miles, the largest freshwater lake in the world has the perfect name: Lake Superior. In fact, it's so huge that it's bounded by 3 U.S. states and 1 Canadian province.

WHAT SKILL are you hugely superior at? (Just don't brag about it to others!)

imagination igniter

— 164 —

IF YOU WERE asked to plan the ultimate trip across America, where would your route meander to get from coast to coast?

165

The Corn Palace in Mitchell, South Dakota, is entirely covered in real cobs of corn!

IF YOU COULD create a building made entirely of a natural product, what would it be made of?

166

IF YOU COULD snap your fingers and instantly travel to 3 different national parks in a single day, which 3 would you want to visit without having to drive to them?

Harley Davidson motorcycles, the most famous around, are manufactured in Milwaukee, Wisconsin.

IF YOU WERE TO spend a week touring a single region of America on a motorcycle, which area would it be?

IF YOU HAD BEEN a pioneer crossing the United States 150 years ago in a covered wagon, what do you think would have been the most difficult part about traveling back then?

169

Oklahoma has an unusual nickname: the Sooner State. It was named after the homesteaders who got a head start on the official beginning of the 1893 land grab and staked their claim "sooner."

IF YOU COULD have gotten any parcel of land in the country simply by staking a claim first, which piece of land would you have wanted to claim?

170

IF YOU COULD redraw the shape of the United States, what would it look like?

171

Each day, more than 50 plays and musicals are performed on Broadway in New York City!

IF YOU COULD create a musical about your family, what kind of music would it feature?

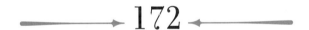

172

IF YOU COULD visit any sports stadium in America, which one would you choose?

→ 173 ←

IF YOU COULD open your own store in Minnesota's Mall of America, the nation's largest mall with 520 stores, what would your particular store feature?

→ 174 ←

IF YOU COULD PUT any message you wanted on a billboard along a busy highway, what would the billboard say? (You can't use more than 10 words, so make each one count!)

175

MT. WASHINGTON in New Hampshire and Lookout Mountain in Tennessee are just a couple of the many famous mountains in the United States. If you were in charge of naming a mountain, what would you name it? (Choose something besides your own name!)

176

IF YOU COULD climb any one thing at all in the United States, what would you choose to scale?

→ 177 ←

At 4,224 feet long, the New River Gorge Bridge in southern West Virginia is the longest spanning, steel single-arch bridge in the world. Each October hundreds of parachutists from around the world jump 876 feet into the gorge!

WITH YOUR safety guaranteed, what would you like to parachute from? Into?

→ 178 ←

IF YOU COULD create the most amazing interstate bridge ever, what would it look like and what would the bridge cross?

AS a PIONEER IN the 1800s, which do you think would be harder to cross with all of your possessions—a swift and deep river or a rocky mountain pass?

IMAGINATION IGNITER

→ 180 ←

IN YOUR OPINION, which would be the most boring 5-hour drive—traveling on a straight road across an empty prairie or on a winding road through a dense forest? Why?

—— → 181 ← ——

During late summer, up to 1.5 million Mexican free-tailed bats make nightly flights from the crevices of the Congress Avenue Bridge in Austin, Texas, as they hunt for food.

IF YOU WERE A BAT, what structure would you want to hang from each night?

—— → 182 ← ——

IF YOU COULD pack only 3 extra nonessential items for a 2-week trip, what would you choose to make your trip complete?

→ 183 ←

When Alabama seceded from the Union in 1861, Winston County reacted by voting to secede from the state.

CAN YOU THINK of one time in your life when a group felt one way about something and you stood firm and decided to do something else?

→ 184 ←

IF YOU COULD choose a new city for your state's capital, what would it be?

IF YOU COULD travel aboard Air Force One with the president of the United States for an hour, what questions would you ask during your flight?

IF YOU COULD have any form of transportation to take you on an adventure, what would you choose?

—— → 187 ← ——

RUGBY, NORTH DAKOTA, is the geographical center of the North American continent. Where exactly is Rugby located? And how far do you live from the geographical center of North America? (Consult an atlas and discover the answers!)

—— → 188 ← ——

IF YOU COULD have your picture taken in front of any famous landmark in the United States, where would you want to be photographed?

189

IN MANY WAYS, both Alaska and Hawaii are very different from the other 48 states. How many things can you think of that make each of these states unusual?

190

EVERY STATE HAS a state flower. Which flower would you choose to represent yourself?

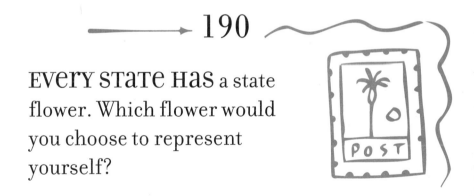

— 191 —

Key West is Florida's southernmost city, yet it is cooler there in the summer than anywhere else in Florida.

WHAT IS ONE thing about you that people wouldn't expect?

— 192 —

WHERE IS THE hottest place you've ever been? The coldest?

193

Along with several other big U.S. cities, Baltimore, Maryland, has a large aquarium to showcase fish from around the world.

IF YOU HaD a 100,000-gallon aquarium, what types of fishes would you want in it?

194

IF YOU COULD take apart any landmark or major structure in the United States and reassemble it somewhere else, what would it be and where would you make its new home?

Imagination Igniter

→ 195 ←

IF YOU HaD TO live in just one state for the rest of your life—and were never able to go beyond its borders—which one would you pick? (No, you can't choose your own state!)

IF YOU COULD DO something to a rest area to make it really cool, what would it be?

CHICAGO'S SEARS TOWER, the nation's tallest building, has 110 floors. If you could live on any floor in the Sears Tower, which one would you choose?

→ 198 ←

OF THE FOLLOWING 5 man-made places, which one would you choose to go to for an unforgettable first-time visit: an architectural marvel, a hall of fame, a haunted house, a lighthouse, or a famous sports stadium?

→ 199 ←

The annual winter carnival in St. Paul, Minnesota, is famous for its large ice sculptures.

IF YOU COULD carve anything from a 20-foot-square block of ice, what would you sculpt?

200

Hastings, Nebraska, is the city in which Kool-Aid was invented back in 1927.

IF YOU COULD create a brand-new flavor for Kool-Aid, what would it be?

201

IF YOU COULD preserve any natural treasure currently being destroyed near your home, which one would you want to save?

202

WHAT IS ONE place, at least at this point in your life, that you have no interest in ever visiting? Why?

203

CAN YOU FIGURE out which state this is from the rhyming riddle below?

I'm the fourth-largest state,
and I've got great mountain rivers.
If you visit me in winter,
you'll have oodles of shivers!

(The answer to this riddle can be found in question 13.)

NOW IT'S YOUR TURN! Write a 4-line rhyming riddle about a state (but make sure you check your facts first!).

_____

_____

_____

_____

(Answer: _____)

Be an armchair traveler! Most states will mail free tourist information to your home. If you could have a copy of any state's official travel guide, which one would you want to find in your mailbox tomorrow morning?

Got a question of your own that you'd like to send us? How about giving us your answer to one or more of the questions in this book? We'd love to hear from you. Write us a letter, put it in the mail, and we'll be sure to get it . . . as long as you address it as follows:

Bret and Paul, The Question Guys™
P.O. BOX 340, YANKTON, SD 57078

MY QUESTIONS:

ABOUT THE AUTHORS

Bret Nicholaus and Paul Lowrie have coauthored twenty books, including the national best-selling question books *The Conversation Piece* and *The Christmas Conversation Piece*. To date, the authors have written more than 3,500 questions designed to ignite creativity in adults and children. Articles about their works have appeared in numerous publications, including *Family Circle*, *Publishers Weekly*, the *Chicago Tribune*, and the *New York Post*. Their books have also been featured on *The View* and *Boy Meets World*. Bret and Paul are graduates of Bethel University, St. Paul, Minnesota, with degrees in communication and marketing, respectively. Nicholaus and his family live in the Chicago area; Lowrie resides in South Dakota. For more information about the authors or their books, please visit their Web site at www.questmarc.com.